Wordglass

Gogol: His Life and Work by Vsevolod Setchkarev
(Translator)
New York: New York University Press, 1965.
London: Peter Owen, 1965.

The Art of Kasak by Nikolai Kasak
(Editor, Translator, Foreword)
with commentaries by Marcello Gallian, Gyula Cosice,
Enrico Prampolini, Sir Herbert Read, James J. Sweeney,
Ted Walik; and an abbreviated version of the artist's
manifesto on physical art.
New York: October House, 1968.

August Sander: Photographs of an Epoch, 1904 – 1959
by August Sander
(Historical Commentary)
with a preface by Beaumont Newhall; in conjunction
with an exhibition at the Philadelphia Museum of Art,
March 1 – April 27, 1980, and elsewhere.
Millerton, NY: Aperture, 1980.

From Action to Dynamic Silence: The Art of Nikolai Kasak
by John E. Bowlt and Nikolai Kasak
(Co-Contributor)
with Nicoletta Misler; in conjunction with The Institute
of Modern Russian Culture.
Salt Lake City, Utah: Charles Schlacks, Jr., 1991.

Wordglass

Poems by

Robert Kramer

POETS WEAR PRADA • Hoboken, New Jersey

Wordglass

First North American Publication 2015

Poets Wear Prada
533 Bloomfield Street
2nd Floor
Hoboken, NJ 07030
http://pwpbooks.blogspot.com/

Grateful acknowledgment is made to the following publications where some of these poems have previously appeared:

Group 74, Home Planet News, HYN, Poets, and Voice Media.

ISBN-13: 978-0615879260
ISBN-10: 0615879268

Printed in the U.S.A.

Front cover image: Caspar David Friedrich, *Der Wanderer über dem Nebelmeer* [Wanderer above the sea of fog], 1818; oil on canvas, 95cm x 75cm; Kunsthalle Hamburg, Germany. Reproduced from http://www.wikipaintings.org (accessed July 29, 2013).

Author photo: Evelyn Fitzgerald, 2006

In loving memory of my wife,
Mary Elizabeth

Table of Contents

Editor's Preface

Robert Kramer has been a habitué of important places. Father, poet, playwright, translator, professor (English, German, Comparative Literature, Art History, International Studies) — *pianiste* and soldier (trained with the 82nd Airborne, Paratroopers) — he first touched ground in New York in 1933 and turned the life of a mind, led, since, in errant step, by ardor of curiosity and scholarly inquiry, to a model of peregrine cerebration usually reserved for explorers, enjoyed by the adventurer, indulged and indulged in by spies, visited as fate, haphazardly, on those, like army *brats*, unsuspecting and indisposed.

Product of American education, eventually furthered in Europe, following military service (commenced in the air) culminating in commission both as a specialist in chemical weaponry and radiation defense, Robert took the divergent path, a more humane approach, toward civilization: gathering advanced degrees, to teach, do research, lecture, and write. Debuting in St. Louis, he traveled downriver in the best literary tradition to New Orleans; the Civil Rights Movement, then, in its earliest stages. Playing piano, nights, in French Quarter cafés and bars, lent peculiarly *academic* aspect to time spent in the classroom, now, inadvertently, his "day job." Daughter Karen furnished further precedent; papers, books, visiting appointments, prizes ensued: from the National Endowment for the Humanities (six), a Fulbright Scholarship for research in Munich, sponsorship by the Swiss government to study in Bern.

Manhattan College brought Robert back from Xavier University and New Orleans to New York: there to extend his octet of specialized variations. All things come down in time. So, *Wordglass* descends, one may say, out of a Phineus Fogg: alighting with delicate ballast, precision, and poise — composure, just slightly antic, befitting an observer, seer transmogrified via such vehicle of *Redone*sque vantage. Perspective thus enriched by broad view, pertinent opportunity, and extemporaneous occasion, once on paper, compels contemplation through monocular aperture: a complex *camera obscura* conjoining accretive knowledge at the point experience succeeds to transcendent perception.

From the first, interpreting Gogol (through German), and Russian thought, rendered in English; assaying diverse elevation — steppe and *stupen* — between that vast influence and the *Brocken*, *strasse*, and *boulevards* (widening with empire) assimilative to nineteenth-century Continental culture, Robert, like one of its heroes, amid bibliographical wanderings of a maturing scholar, accumulated species particular to a hypothetical individual *type*, whose consciousness, strivings, strengths, sufferings, and consolation emerged beside fragments attesting an earlier and still-potential grandeur, long concealed, *christ*ened, ultimately, neither without significance nor some irony, as the "Renaissance." Bonds suspended by "Reformation" and "Enlightenment" catch at the height of "German Romanticism"; landscapes revealed that cry out for themselves, seeming to sight along subterfuge of "Symbolist" ravines, to the "Surreal"; then, final decadence of Weimar, when the universal freedom conceived, together with a found autonomy of acknowledgeable unconscious, broke with the *real*, so-called reality avail of all integration. Consolidated, shared belief capitulated to the enormity of human suffering.

Some sense of commonly held vantage, mutual venture, and anointed value inhere beneath the lens of *Wordglass*. Gogol albeit hardly unique in elaborating fantasy to heighten introspection submitted for public view might well have led the "Moderns" nevertheless to tease significance, evince metonymic epiphany, from the reverie of usual objects. The fissioning of the individual — whether by overt compromise or attrition of characteristic, psychological, functional; or by stasis of statistical suspense in regard to (rather, disrespect for) human utility versus demographic use; with reality relegated to randomness among numbers only occasionally bearing integral value — devolves on all unqualified to serve the hieratic championship of the objective as motive, de facto *ars poetica* and golem, sustaining refusal of the atomized subject to go gentle into that good nonentity.

Maker of thousandfold translation, the poet of *Wordglass* brings news. Ascent in knowledge and imagination adverts to the luminous findings, trove of exploration and high adventure, returning with crystal in hand; its prism, these pages. The livid apostrophes of Rilke, Trakl's dreamsongs — recur, their manifest perception self-similar: further refined, descried experience successive circumstance differentiates; manner of speech, renewed, comprehends: alike, bequeath. Robert Kramer extends the authority of personal vision beyond synthesis of past and present, both unprecedented and not, to include not only his but ours, preliminary to a light not our own.

John "Jack" Jackie (Edward) Cooper

Wordglass

The Search for Egg Island

To see patterns in the trees,
faces in the foliage —
and then to lose them,
as one who seeks his father's voice
among tangled yards of tape
(when memory fails,
and only memory of memory remains —
from tangled years lost) ...

Searching the darkness,
headlights strike the rain,
meeting with soft resistance.
As they weave through the fog,
their twisting beams lash out.
Drilling mineshafts through
the mighty mountain of night,
twin cones pursue a winding vein's
unknown course to the final core,
into the heart of the black mountain.

Reminder

Your blue-haired aunt
reminds you of something you lived through
as a small blond child,
but which you cannot recollect —
though you struggle to remember.
Insistently and in detail,
with weaving red-tipped fingers,
she reconstructs those moments —
the falling snow, the pulled-down shade,
that pungent odor — until all come alive for you,
but believable only as the experiences
of another — yet painful — still gaps, losses
that you can never totally recover,
repressed, made alien,
stolen by oblivion,
as implausible now
as what the frog's eye
tells the frog's brain.

As My Daughter Screamed in the Night

From my predawn dream
I was awakened
by a sudden scream from hers:
first, fragment from without
intruding into my nocturnal world of sleep,
then the final note
still piercing from her bedroom,
as I stumbled through darkness
(toenail scraping chairs)
to her bedside,
felt her body taut and trembling.
Reassuring, with words banal,
I clasped her hands in mine.
Her fists, so tightly clenched,
relaxed; her heaving chest grew calm.
She, still half-asleep,
said, "Goodnight, Daddy."
I smiled in the darkness, hoped
she'd passed the worst of her nightmare —

and I returned to mine.

A Child Under the Moon in the Wet Grass
Searching for Night Crawlers, the Very First Time

The spell of a summer night
transforms a lawn —
by day sun bright and languid
to teeming life beneath the moon:
a child
in the wet grass
searching for night crawlers —
the very first time;
the uncle with a bobbing flashlight,
on his knees, and feeling through the grass;
the empty Campbell's soup can poised;
the searching beam ...

Then to see, within that shaft of light,
the great pink worms — so fat,
and slowly curling from beneath the tufts of grass —
as they rise wriggling from
their hidden world of dark-in-day,
to coil round the child's white fingers.
And thus, to know
that, all the while,
under the placid sunlit surface,
something cool and moist is breeding.

And so, I gaze, now,
on your earnest human face,
and see concealed beneath your cheek
— from within my Röntgen mind —
the double rows of teeth
that curve along the jawbone,
ascending to each ear,
and grinning in the dark.

Alma Reading

Outside the window
faint patters
as of gusts of rain
and turning leaves,
or windfalls.
I watch you read
before the mirror:
your eyes move
in communion with the page,
like Alice looking into
the enclosed garden —
the unattainable rose garden —
the site of the mystic marriage;
and then as one
who lies alone in the dark,
blanket to her throat,
and from bed listens
to loud laughter in the next room
or the sounds of conjoined lovers
moving rhythmically
beyond the next wall;
these memories of childhood:
a ray of light falling through the blinds
to give a glimpse of your parents' bed —
or, seen through a slightly opened door,
a silk stocking on a fleshy thigh —
or a door suddenly slammed
to hide a mother's turning nakedness.
And a child dreams
that her hands
are turning into claws.

Your fingers tremble.

Hamburg Zoo, 1943

The elephant is on fire
at the Hamburg zoo:
futile shrieks from behind
the undersized eyes
that blink and roll
as the red American phosphorus
smokes and singes,
burning into the flesh.

Wide-eyed children
emerge from the darkness,
gather around him.
Ragged,
they stare in silence
as he rears and coils his tail
upon himself,
flings himself —
onto his back —
tossing, writhing —
to mute the flame that sears
the red mass of his innards —
his legs kicking
baggy trousers
of loose gray skin,
while his small eyes roll.

The firemen, shouting, in black slickers,
drag the gray hose before him,
but the pressure fails —
the pipes breached —
as flames from the burning city
lick at the night sky,
the smoke smarts the eyes,
and searchlights finger the darkness above.

And the keeper, weeping,
runs up with buckets of water,
splashes them over the gray mass
that shrieks and writhes and steams,
until the Gestapo arrives —
six shots — silence —
the acrid scent
of gushed urine —
as the sirens sound again.

Bergson on the Staircase

Recall:
the chilling instant
when you must pause
on the descending staircase
— suddenly — to know
all your being is concentrated
into this single point of space and time,
and that this alone is real — this briefest moment —
increment between the past and future —
when the fragile body floats
— suspended at its own gravity —
between one step
and the next.

This thought resounds
within the skull
like echoes of your voice
— solitary —
in a Pyrenean cavern.
No other voice confirms
your own reality.
You, now, are poised
on the crest of Time's fiercely breaking wave.

A Parisian Love

In this preening and seductive city,
with its babbling houses and whispering fountains,
sun-bright squares, and sparrows perched
on the shoulders of equestrian statues
— amid all the intricate alleys
that make up its maze —
she loves things coarse and pungent:
through her fingers — stout brown bristly cord;
in a closet — the scent of camphor.

But this Parisian woman also sees,
deeply, into her learned lover's mind:
how this woman came to him
— a library of books made flesh —
odor, moisture, ennui and fatigue
leading to satisfied desire
but also to the veiled distaste
of things concealed, humid and mucous
— each month a bleeding —
her unconscious body
with a secret and perilous life of its own —
threatening, perhaps too free in its existence
outside of his brain and his verbal domination.

Raimund on Stage in Vienna

You, the director,
stand somewhere
in the dark of the empty theater;
I, the actor,
crouch on stage
in full light,
facing your darkness.

My lunge and veer project
ambivalence and ambiguity,
amid this desolate lethargy —
this languorous vertigo.

For, beneath this ancient city,
the earth is hollow:
cellars and vaults, abandoned tunnels,
moldy crypts, catacombs and canals,
subterranean streams,
and labyrinthine sewers
of floating filth.

My furnishings, but mirror, mask and stage:
I live like a dream in the sandstorm
of the hourglass.
And yet, the small epiphanies.

For like Nerval's lobster,
led through the streets
on a blue silk ribbon,
I am an incorrigible walker of labyrinths.

The Exile

You are as mad
as one alone in a foreign land
of fall and fog,
who drinks his gin by chance
in a smoke-filled bar,
never-before visited,
in the backstreets of an unknown city,
and who, when the phone rings, straightens up,
expecting the call to be for him;
who, walking through crowded streets,
perceives — across the evening traffic —
his father's face — long lost;
or who on nights of unshared bed
— after twenty years —
still dreams of her — the one he once had loved,
in puberty and summer sand —
and wakens — torn with longing.

You are as lost
in the winter-morning sunbeams'
moment of disorientation as
one who wakes from a dream
not knowing where he is, nor with whom,
nor in what room, what city, what land.

Absurd red bushes branch, now,
from the corners of your eyes,
but no songbirds perch there.

Hesitation
An Erotic Interlude

Pale blue veins
in the crease of the groin.
White crystal surf,
frozen — on verge of shatter —
glazes the gray glass cliffs
of the green glass mountain.
The wind rests in yellow.
A buzzing fly dances
on the watery eye of an ox.

In a labyrinth of flowers:
the shadow of a dream —
the dream — of the shadow.

Did ever a lemming look back?

Summit

On penthouse terrace,
in darkness pierced by blades of light,
well-past midnight, facing east
toward the moonlight-glossy river
and bridge-strands of beaded light.
So high, the city's gaseous sounds
are dampened now
to muffled roar
— like the breath of a sleeping beast —
as a thrumming bass persists within,
beneath tinkling glasses and
screamlike female laughter.
At this chartless crossing
of space and time
— cooled by night wind —
stone parapets,
beneath your fingers,
seem to yield and sway.

Your eyes are tempted
downward — like a climber's —
one who has emerged from behind
the craggy alpine spine
after vertical ascent
onto the face of heavy snow,
and then to the shock of nothing above
but gray scudding clouds,
as the sudden blast
of unchecked chilling winds
almost tears his fingers
from the narrow summit's ice;
behind tinted glasses,
his eyes squint closed.

Your Voice Keeps on Talking ...

Your voice keeps on talking
after you have stopped,
like centrifugal ripples in a pond
after the flung stone;
and the language you dream in
is not the language you speak.

And, thus, in tea rooms and palm courts,
with marble floors
and solitary great clocks,
you seek what is most valid,
most elusive,
amid teacups and martinis,
trembling in the veined hands
of elegant women with blue hair
and too-rouged cheek

as they laugh with gleaming artificial teeth
and the affection of an octopus
for a bat.

Bernhard's Circular Monologue

Starfish, ferns and scallop shells,
an octopus — my mind —
a stage magician's trunk
with trapdoors underneath
and secret drawers;
and yet, those scattered moments
when the mirror of the mind
is briefly focused
on its own uncanny depths,
reflecting on hidden processes,
though soon to be directed elsewhere,
as the dark forces persist,
unseen, unheard,
barely discerned
by the sleeping geometrician
and his sleeping theorems;
or by her who stands aghast
on a hotel balcony in Majorca,
overlooking a garden
split between the brilliance
of the late afternoon sun
and the shadow of this oblong block
with its cool geometric severity;
and when they ask Nerval why,
he answers:
"because it does not bark
and knows the secrets of the sea."

Between Waves

I

The dull boom and hiss
of ocean waves against the shore
leave scattered shells
of clam and scallop,
strings of pea-green kelp,
iridescent discs
of glass-and-lilac jellyfish
on the gray sand,
as the swirling sheet
of white foam
recedes.

II

Enter the seaside cottage,
this cool September noon.
Let the patched screen door
spring shut behind you.
See the translucent white curtain
across the opened window
flutter in the breeze;
the azure pitcher on a tray,
surrounded by its sea-green glasses
(its chipped side,
in the mirror, visible).
As your city shoes
grind forgotten grains
of sand, unseen,
into the varnished
wooden floorboards,
her fingers will brush
the crisp spread upon the bed.

III

Even as the striding sandpipers
dart on pencil legs
across the wet sand
— barely abandoned by the wave —
to plunge their pointed beaks
into their tiny prey,
another wave crashes
and subsides,
to leave behind
a stranded mass
of white and frothing foam,
quivering in the wind
like some enormous albino jellyfish
from the alien and primeval seas.

The Blind Man by the Sea

The blind man listens, very carefully,
to the sounds of the sea,
listens so long and with such care
that at any instant he can tell
what occurs where in every span
of the waters invisible before him.
Seated, facing the sea, he knows
to his right a wave has now just crashed
from its overhanging rim, and
that directly in front of him
a rushing sound reports
a wave already fallen,
flattened and approaching;
and to his left
a wave's last gasp soughs and sighs,
as that wave washes up onto the beach
to the limit and recedes;
and once again his ears shift
to the heavy boom and dash
as the next wave breaks,
doubling, tripling, as if fragmented,
the pitch rising higher
until a final dying hiss
before his feet.
"Green sea, white foam," the blind man says.

Dancers on a Falling Bridge

Like jugglers in the snow
or dancers on a falling bridge,
we seek to toss and cling
between our bed and clock.
At times your heart seems closed
as the leather eye
of a camel in the sandstorm,
but I watch for the flicker of your eye
— a canary in the mineshaft —
your amber eye,
embedded in your olive skin.

And in the moon of our melancholy
— this pitch and warp of earth —
like truant children trapped on high
by noonday's clanging steeple bells,
we feel a nausea of ear, a nausea of eye.
We listen to each other in the dark,
saliva gathering in the basin of the mouth —
no word spoken.

Penelope Revisited

Upon your arrival home,
in the gray foredawn,
your key does not fit the lock:
confident, at first,
you check the key,
reverse its teeth,
press in deeper,
withdraw slightly,
tilt and twist —
then sense your sweat
when all to no avail —
the door before you, now,
strangely alien.

Under the time lens,
in a world of fragments ...

On Her Departure

As you observe her slowly walking away,
you feel the time elapse
between the foot that rises —
foot that falls ...
adrift in space ...
as when, in the trance of solar noon,
from forest floor,
you watch a great blue butterfly
float off slowly
between the trees;
its pulsing wings,
fine-veined and delicate,
contract — expand —
in languid silence,
vanish into woodland depths,
as in an emerald world
beneath the sea.

Lassitude, disquieting,
as when you respond, warmly,
to a beckoning hand,
a smile, an invitation —
intended not for you
but rather for one behind you —
and so must avert your eyes
with the shame of your presumption.

As foolish and as melancholy now
as at the circus sideshow —
the fetus of that six-footed calf
floating in formaldehyde.

Late Love

As in a tattered, nearly forgotten notebook —
the telephone numbers of dead men:

With lush thighs
and elegantly curving calves,
her slender ankles
embrace me,
and though our lashes brush
and tongues entwine —
this is already the past.

Yesterday's yearning,
the rose in the skull.

A Little Tiny Love Poem

As on a Sunday evening
by an ocean long ago,
amid the lengthening shadows of the sinking sun
and the camphor scent of white Noxzema,
as I dig a tunnel through the cool damp sand
beneath our castle with its spiral turrets:
the pleasure of breaking through
that final barrier,
to twine our two sandy fingers —
yours,
tunneling from the other side.

The Archaeologist to His Glass

As the last drummer boy marches in his shroud
across the empty world —
still, I strive to decipher
random letters from faded inscriptions —
splinters of forgotten revelations —
late afternoon sunlight
through a half-empty sherry glass;
or in a waterfront bar,
the babbled tales of a drunken sailor.

But who is that lost ferryman
drifting in my blue veins?
While in these closed bottles,
cheering spirits from warmer climes dwell,
waiting in their crystal cells like lovely nuns
full of yearning for their thirsty lovers?
Until I sip my nightshade, a pale belladonna,
to dissolve
like a diamond in goat's blood,
and wipe away
this clutch of cobwebs over bone dust,
this taste of ash?

Orpheus
The Descent into the Underworld

A wisp of perfume in the night air —
and you wander the twisting streets
of the ancient city,
as they grow ever more narrow,
following their descending turns
into ever greater blackness,
past heaps of coiled hemp;
the reek of turpentine, pitch and tar;
past silent crumbling churches;
the scents of spices, fish and urine;
past another seaman —
his back to you, hands up
against a wall, head down,
his back and shoulders convulsing.
You pass the last flickering lights
of upper stories,
the quick scurry of rats
in the shadows,
the cobblestones that lump and pitch
beneath your feet.
You sense the nearness of the water,
breathe the briny air of the harbor,
the red wine still on your lips,
your member rigid to the navel,
impelled as in a dream
to seek that first and final darkness.

Acknowledgments

The author extends his thanks to the following publications where some of these poems first appeared, sometimes in slightly different format:

Group 74	"As My Daughter Screamed in the Night"
Home Planet News	"A Child Under the Moon in the Wet Grass"
HYN	"Penelope Revisited"
Poets	"The Search for Egg Island"
Voice Media	"Hesitation"

About the Author

A native New Yorker and former Director of the New York Poets Cooperative, Robert Kramer studied and lived in Europe as First Lieutenant of the Unites States Army, Fulbright Scholar in Munich, Germany, and as Swiss Government Fellow in Bern, Switzerland, returning to the United States to teach at the university level.

He is the author of numerous books and articles on the history of literature and art, and has taught Art History and Literature at St. Louis University, Xavier University of Louisiana, and Manhattan College. He has also been a visiting professor at the University of Connecticut, Syracuse University, and Haverford College. An expert on Art History, receiving six awards from the National Endowment for the Humanities, he has lectured at the Smithsonian Institute, the Whitney Museum of American Art, and the Art Therapists Association.

A widely published playwright, poet, and translator of European literature, he has read his poetry and translations on radio and television on both coasts, as well as at Harvard, Princeton, and New York Universities.

The former Director of International Studies at Manhattan College, Riverdale, New York, he continues to teach there as Professor of Art History.

A NOTE ON THE TYPE

This book is set in Cambria, a serif typeface designed by Dutch typographer Jelle Bosma in 2004, for Microsoft, with input from Steve Matteson and Robin Nicholas. Cambria employs very even spacing and proportions, and is characterized by relatively strong vertical and diagonal strokes, contrasting thinner horizontal ones and its smaller horizontal serifs which emphasize stroke endings rather than stand out themselves. These design elements make it a fine choice for on-screen reading and allow it to look good even when printed at small sizes. However it has been criticized as too monotonous to work well for long works of printed text. Despite this shortcoming, Cambria has been widely adopted by the scientific community. Its regular weight has been extended to include many scientific and mathematical symbols.

Cambria is featured in the Microsoft ClearType Font Collection, a set of six fonts developed by exploiting leading-edge technology and embodying best in design practice to provide readable, attractive typefaces for either traditional print or on-screen use. ClearType, first introduced with Windows Vista and Office 2007, continues to be distributed with all newer versions of Office, various free Office viewers, the Microsoft Office Compatibility Pack, and the Open XML File Format Converter for Mac.

www.ingramcontent.com/pod-product-compliance
Lightning Source LLC
Chambersburg PA
CBHW021916040426
42447CB00007B/888

* 9 7 8 0 6 1 5 8 7 9 2 6 0 *